GRaphic
Novel

AVI

W9-BXY-247

DISCARD

HPHS Library

CITY OF LIGHT,
CITY OF DARK

OCT 05

A RICHARD JACKSON BOOK

CITY OF LIGHT, CITY OF DARK

A COMIC-BOOK NOVEL

story by **AVI**

art by **BRIAN FLOCA**

Orchard Books New York

Text copyright © 1993 by Avi
Illustrations copyright © 1993 by Brian Floca
Spanish translation by José Aranda and Anthony Trujillo
First Orchard Paperbacks edition 1995
All rights reserved. No part of this book may be reproduced
or transmitted in any form or by any means, electronic or
mechanical, including photocopying, recording, or by any
information storage or retrieval system, without permission
in writing from the Publisher.

Orchard Books, 95 Madison Avenue,
New York, NY 10016

Manufactured in the United States of America
Book design by Mina Greenstein
The text of this book is hand lettered. The illustrations are
rendered in pen and india ink applied with a brush.

Hardcover   10 9 8 7 6 5 4 3
Paperback   10 9 8 7 6 5 4 3 2 1

Library of Congress Cataloging-in-Publication Data
Avi, date. City of light, city of dark : a comic-book novel / story
by Avi; art by Brian Floca.   p.   cm. "A Richard Jackson book."
Summary: Asterel races against time to locate a token which
will prevent the Kurbs from freezing the city.
ISBN 0-531-06800-5 (tr.)   ISBN 0-531-08650-X (lib. bdg.)
ISBN 0-531-07058-1 (pbk.)
[1. Fantasy. 2. Cartoons and comics.]   I. Floca, Brian, ill.
II. Title.   PN6727.A95C57   1993   741.5′973—dc20   93-2887

For Shaun and Kevin
— AVI

For my parents
— B.F.

These Kurbs owned an Island as well as the sky above it. And with their POWER they controlled both day and night. For Kurbs have always thrived in darkness, turning to the dark as moths turn to light.

Years ago, when People first came to the Kurbs' Island, they wanted to build themselves a City there. First, however, they had to ask permission of the Kurbs. To this request the Kurbs' leader replied,

PEOPLE! THE LAND YOU WISH TO BUILD ON BELONGS TO US, THE **KURBS.** STILL, WE ARE WILLING TO **LEND** YOU THIS ISLAND AS WELL AS OUR **POWER** SO YOU MAY HAVE THE LIGHT AND WARMTH YOU HUMANS REQUIRE. **BUT THERE IS A PRICE.** EACH YEAR YOU **MUST** ENACT A RITUAL TO SHOW YOU ACKNOWLEDGE THAT THIS ISLAND REMAINS **OURS** AND IS GOVERNED BY **OUR** RULES. IF YOU **FAIL** TO PERFORM THIS RITUAL —BE WARNED! —THE CONSEQUENCES FOR YOU WILL BE ***DIRE!***

To this pronouncement the People listened and finally agreed. So the Kurbs established—

The Treaty of
THE RITUAL CYCLE OF ACKNOWLEDGMENT
THAT THIS ISLAND BELONGS
TO THE KURBS

Whereas:

1) Each year, on the 21st day of June, the Kurbs shall hide their POWER somewhere in some form in the People's City.

2) The People will have six months to search for it.

3) When the People find the POWER, they shall return it to a place of safekeeping, designated by the Kurbs, no later than noon on the 21st day of December.

4) If the POWER is *not* returned, the City will grow so dark and so cold that it will *freeze*.

5) And the Kurbs will take their Island back.

Furthermore:

6) From the moment the Kurbs hide their POWER on the 21st of June, the hours of City daylight shall begin to decrease.

7) When the POWER is ritually returned to its place of safekeeping on the 21st of December, City days shall start to grow warm. The hours of daylight will lengthen.

Finally:

8) THE RITUAL CYCLE OF ACKNOWLEDGMENT marks two halves of the human year, December to June, June to December. For the first six months the POWER shall be kept safe in a place designated by the Kurbs. For the second six months the POWER will be hidden somewhere in the city, and the People must search for it. Should the People fail to find the POWER and return it, the Cycle will be broken and the People's lease on this island shall be ended *forever*.

AGREED _____   AGREED _____
For the People   For the Kurbs

Signed on the 45th day of the 13th moon, Kurb year 55122337.

In the early years of this agreement the Kurbs' POWER was hidden in an ear of corn, then a musket ball. Later it was put in an oil lamp. Most recently the POWER has been put within a transit token, the small golden disk used by the People as fare for bus or subway travel.

Who searches for this POWER?

The People chose a woman. She alone had the responsibility of conducting the search. To help her in her searching, the People gave her powers that included special sight.

Now, when this woman had a daughter, the first thing she did was give that girl those powers. Only when the girl was older did her mother provide her with knowledge of the search as well as her future responsibilities. This meant that when the woman died, there was someone new to take up the yearly search. Thus, THE RITUAL CYCLE OF ACKNOWLEDGMENT continued, mother to daughter, mother to daughter, generation after generation.

Now, the means by which the woman passed on her special powers was simple: the POWER—in whatever its form—was held to the baby's forehead. From that moment the daughter was fated to take on the searcher's responsibilities.

For hundreds of years the cycle of seeking the POWER and of returning it to the safekeeping of the Kurbs continued unbroken. Then, eleven years ago, something very different happened.

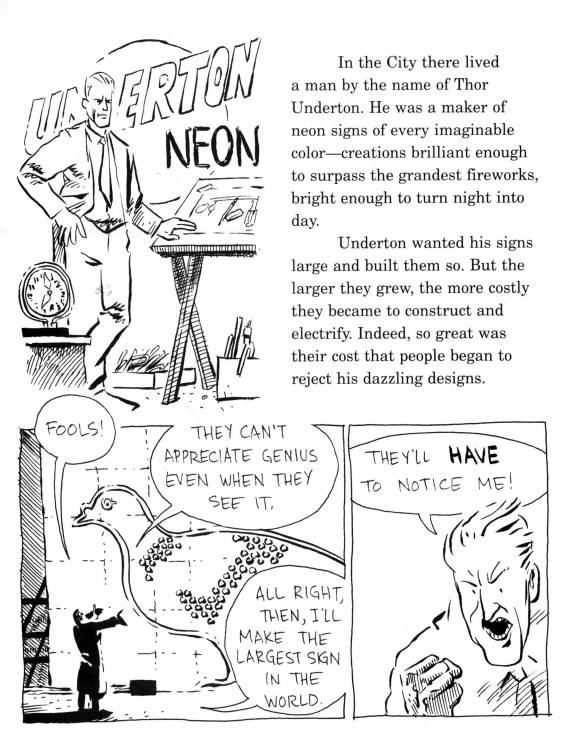

In the City there lived a man by the name of Thor Underton. He was a maker of neon signs of every imaginable color—creations brilliant enough to surpass the grandest fireworks, bright enough to turn night into day.

Underton wanted his signs large and built them so. But the larger they grew, the more costly they became to construct and electrify. Indeed, so great was their cost that people began to reject his dazzling designs.

Underton set to work with the assistance of his young apprentice, one Theodore Bitner.

Underton had found Theo abandoned on a dark city street. He took him in, fed and clothed him, and taught him much about sign making and electricity. Naturally, Theo wished to please Underton.

After much time and many difficulties, Underton—with Theo's help—completed his masterwork—the largest neon sign ever attempted—a gigantic spectacle of sparkling, blazing, blinking, flashing color. Its letters read,

Underton considered atomic power, solar power, sea power, wind power—nothing was enough.

Frantic, he spent hours in libraries. He consulted the Moderns. He studied the Ancients. In so doing he stumbled upon the history of the Kurbs and *their* POWER.

Further research revealed that in recent times this POWER resided in a City transit token.

But would Underton be able to find the one token from among the millions of tokens that existed? He looked for a year but did not find it.

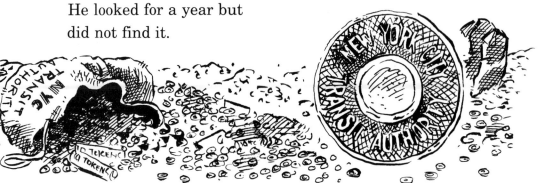

Then he learned that, at that time, the person whose mission it was to search for the token was a young woman named Asterel. He would wait until *she* found the small golden disk. Then, *before* she could restore the token to its place of safekeeping, he would take it and thus gain control of the Kurbs' POWER!

Slyly, Underton confided in Theo about the Kurbs, the POWER, and THE RITUAL CYCLE OF ACKNOWLEDGMENT.

FURTHER

THEO, IF I ASKED YOU TO DO SOMETHING A BIT UNUSUAL, YOU'D BE WILLING TO DO IT, WOULDN'T YOU?

OH, YES, SIR! IT'S THE LEAST I COULD DO.

THEO, THAT SEARCHER OF THE **POWER** I TOLD YOU ABOUT ROAMS THE CITY IN DISGUISE. IN OLDEN TIMES SHE MIGHT HAVE BEEN A MILKMAID OR CHIMNEY SWEEP.

THE ONE WHO HAS THE JOB THESE DAYS, THIS ASTEREL, HAS PRETENDED TO BE A POLICE WOMAN, A BUS DRIVER, A STREET CLEANER.

WHAT IS SHE THIS YEAR?

METER MAID.

THEO, I WANT YOU TO WATCH HER. FOLLOW HER. BEFRIEND HER. AND WHEN SHE FINDS THE TOKEN – AHEM –

TAKE IT.

17

Theo had no trouble meeting Asterel: he merely parked a car by a fire hydrant. She—a meter maid—gave him a parking ticket. But once the young man and young woman met, they came to like each other. What's more, in the course of time, from January to February, they fell in love.

But the more deeply Theo and Asterel loved, the greater grew their fear that the truth of their identities, if discovered, would split them apart. So they held fast to their secrets—he to the nature of his assignment from Underton, she to her fated mission as the searcher of the POWER.

In the month of March, they married.

Three months after the marriage—at the moment of noon on the 21st of June—Asterel secretly resumed that year's mission of searching for the token hidden by the Kurbs. Theo—just as secretly—spied on her, so he knew when she found the token. But he did not know why his wife slipped off to an underground hideaway beneath the City's Grand Central Station. Though he followed her there, he was unable to see her conceal the token in a hiding place of her own. The truth is, Asterel was to have a baby in December and she needed to keep the token so as to anoint the unborn child. Of that, Theo knew nothing.

In the third week of December, Asterel gave birth to a girl. "Let's name her Estella," she told Theo happily. "The word means 'star.'"

By the morning of the 21st of December, Asterel had regained enough strength to make some excuse to her husband, then slip away to her underground hideaway and fetch the token. With it she intended to anoint her daughter, passing on to Estella the searcher's gift of special sight.

Token in hand to anoint Estella, Asterel returned to the home she shared with Theo. There she found a note:

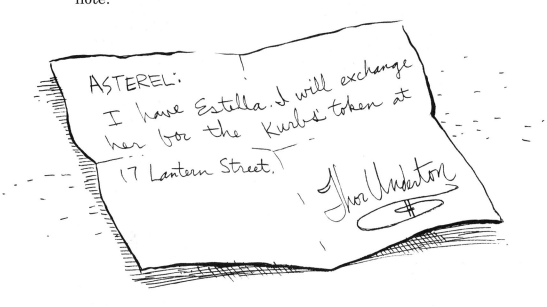

In rage and panic, Asterel raced to Underton's workshop. Instead of bargaining with the genius of light, she commenced to destroy his great sign, shattering the neon tubes into a million slivers of glass. When Underton tried to stop her and save his masterwork, he was accidentally blinded.

Now Asterel faced a terrible decision: should she complete the ritual of the token or set off to search for her baby? She felt she had no choice. She must save the city. In agony she fled the workshop, struggled through the City, and restored the token to its place of safekeeping. Then she fairly flew back to Lantern Street. But Underton, Theo, and her Estella were nowhere to be seen.

That was eleven years ago. In the time since—

Asterel has continued to do as she was meant to do—search for the token and complete the annual ritual. *But she has never stopped looking for her daughter.*

Theo has cared for Estella as lovingly as any father could. But, fearful that Asterel might find him and take their child, he has changed his name, disguised his face, and meekly given over control of his life to Underton. *Above all, he has tried to stay hidden from Asterel.*

As for Underton, he, embittered by blindness, has grown more and more obsessed about the token. Absolutely convinced that its POWER can restore his sight, he devotes all his time, energy, and genius to one goal: *that the token shall be his!*

25

1ST CHAPTER

THE CITY, THE AFTERNOON OF DECEMBER NINETEENTH.

THE JUAREZ FAMILY - CHILDREN, PARENTS, UNCLES, AUNTS, GRANDPARENTS, AND COUSINS - ARE ALL CHEERFULLY EXHAUSTED FROM EATING TOO MUCH. AMONG THE EXHAUSTED ONES IS CARLOS. HE'S SITTING ALONE NEAR A SLIDING DOOR OVERLOOKING A SMALL BALCONY.

WHAT CARLOS SEES OUTSIDE UPSETS HIM.

FOR THE VIEW CONTAINS EVERYTHING HE HATES ABOUT THE CITY: IT'S BLEAK, UGLY, AND BORING.

AS CARLOS WATCHES, A SCRUFFY SPARROW FLITS THROUGH THE AIR. THE BOY SIGHS. FLYING IS THE WAY HE PLANS TO FLEE THE CITY AND GO HOME, WHERE IT'S WARM AND GREEN.

SOON... SOON.

AS CARLOS WATCHES THE SPARROW...

28

THOSE PIGEONS ARE TRYING TO KILL THAT BIRD!

CARLOS TEARS THROUGH THE APARTMENT, OUT THE FRONT DOOR, DOWN THE ELEVATOR, THROUGH THE REVOLVING DOORS, OUT ONTO THE PLAZA.

HEY! STOP!

BUT CARLOS HAS COME TOO LATE.

SAFE WITHIN THE BUILDING, CARLOS CATCHES HIS BREATH. THE BIRDS HAVE TORN HIS SHIRT. HE FEELS BLOOD ON HIS CHEEK.

WHAT MADE THOSE PIGEONS SO FEROCIOUS?

HE LOOKS AT THE DISK HE HAS TAKEN FROM THE DEAD BIRD.

WHAT'S THE BIG DEAL? JUST AN ORDINARY TOKEN.

IS THAT MAN LOOKING FOR ME?

CAN'T BE— HE'S BLIND.

IN THE BEDROOM CARLOS PUTS ON HIS JACKET TO KEEP THE TEARS IN HIS SHIRT FROM BEING SEEN, THEN TURNS UP THE COLLAR TO HIDE HIS SCRATCHES.

HOLA, MAMÁ.

"HI, MOM."

CARLOS! ME TEMO QUE TENEMOS QUE IRNOS PRONTO A CASA.

"CARLOS! I'M AFRAID WE HAVE TO GO HOME SOON."

¿PUEDO MIRAR EL FINAL DE ESTO? ES ACERCA DE LOS PRIMEROS AEROPLANOS.

POR SUPUESTO.

"SURE."

"CAN I WATCH THE END OF THIS? IT'S ABOUT EARLY AIRPLANES."

I'LL FLY FARTHER THAN THEY DID.

MEANWHILE, THE BAG LADY REACHES GRAND CENTRAL STATION....

SIGH...

34

NOW SHE IS HERSELF AGAIN— ASTEREL, THE TOKEN SEARCHER.

WHO HAS THE TOKEN?

SHE MAKES A FIST.

IT'S THIS BOY WHO HAS IT.

ONLY THIRTY-SIX HOURS BEFORE THE DEADLINE. IF I DON'T PUT THAT TOKEN WHERE THE KURBS WANT IT, THE CITY WILL FREEZE!

FIND THE BOY! BUT THE CITY HAS MILLIONS OF BOYS. IF I DO FIND HIM, HOW WILL I GET IT FROM HIM? I'M TIRED OF BEING THE ONLY ONE DOING THIS JOB!

I WISH I COULD SEE ESTELLA.

BUT I DON'T KNOW WHAT SHE LOOKS LIKE ANYMORE AND I CAN SEE ONLY PEOPLE I KNOW — OR THE ONE WHO HOLDS THE TOKEN.

YES, I MUST FIND THAT BOY.

IN A LUMBERING CITY BUS...
CARLOS AND HIS MOTHER SIT IN
THE BACK ROW. AS HIS MOTHER DOZES,
CARLOS REACHES INTO HIS POCKET
AND PULLS THE TOKEN OUT, CURLING
HIS FINGERS OVER IT.

O'Leary's

PHNOM PENH
CAMBODIAN CUIS.

STARTLED BY THE SUDDEN LIGHT, CARLOS
SHOVES THE TOKEN BACK INTO HIS POCKET.
IT BECOMES DARK AGAIN.

YAWN!
MUST BE
TIRED.

CARLOS SLEEPS.

UNSEEN BY THE BOY...

TWO HOURS LATER...

THE DOORWAY, SKOTOS.

YE—

MR. UNDERTON!

LET ME IN, STUBBS.

CLICK

I THOUGHT YOU SAID IT WOULD BE DANGEROUS FOR YOU TO COME HERE.

HAS SOMETHING...

PRIVATE

HAS SOMETHING HAPPENED?

39

DON'T WORRY. I'LL TELL HER NOTHING ABOUT YOUR PAST. JUST HAVE HER READY AT SIX O'CLOCK TOMORROW MORNING.

I'LL BE OUTSIDE YOUR DOOR.

MR. UNDERTON, SIR, SALES HAVEN'T BEEN VERY GOOD AND, IN CONSIDERATION OF THE HOLIDAY SEASON, I WAS—

OUR AGREEMENT WAS SIMPLE. YOU PROVIDE ME WITH TEN PERCENT OF YOUR EARNINGS, OR I INFORM ASTEREL WHERE YOU LIVE. THE **LEAST** THAT WOMAN WOULD DO IS TAKE THE GIRL FROM YOU.

AND NOW TO BUSINESS...

THEO!

I HAVE MONEY!

PRIVA

NO! PLEASE!

THAT'S BETTER. YOU'RE SAFE FOR ANOTHER TWO WEEKS. NOW LET ME OUT.

IT GETS WORSE AND WORSE.

I WISH I COULD TELL SARAH THE TRUTH.

41

IN APARTMENT 7C, 103 110TH STREET...

RECUERDA QUE MAÑANA VOY A JERSEY PARA VER A TÍA NINA QUE ESTÁ ENFERMA. REGRESARÉ EL MIÉRCOLES.

QUISIERA IR CONTIGO. ESTA CIUDAD ES SUCIA Y ME ABURRE.

"NOW REMEMBER, TOMORROW I'M GOING TO JERSEY TO SEE SICK AUNT NINA. BE BACK WEDNESDAY."

"WISH I COULD GO. THIS CITY'S JUST DIRT AND DULLNESS."

LA MAMÁ DE TOM ESPERA QUE VAYAS A QUEDARTE CON ELLOS. TE LLAMARÉ ALLÍ POR LA NOCHE. ¿TIENES DINERO PARA EL AUTOBÚS?

"TOM'S MOTHER IS EXPECTING YOU TO STAY WITH THEM. I'LL CALL YOU THERE TOMORROW NIGHT. YOU HAVE BUS MONEY?"

TENGO UNA FICHA. ¿HAS VISTO ESA REVISTA CON UN PLANEADOR DE MANOS?

FIJÁTE QUE NO.

"A TOKEN. HAVE YOU SEEN THAT MAGAZINE WITH THE HANG GLIDER IN IT?"

"AFRAID NOT."

UNDERTON LIVES IN A FORTY·STORY BUILDING AT THE BOTTOM OF THE CITY.

THAT NIGHT THE BLIND MAN CANNOT SLEEP. HE PROWLS THE BUILDING, WANDERING THROUGH EMPTY ROOMS AND DESERTED FLOORS. EVERYWHERE HE GOES, SKOTOS FOLLOWS. FROM TIME TO TIME UNDERTON STOPS AND FACES THE OUTER GLASS WALLS. BEYOND THEM, HE KNOWS, IS THE CITY. THOUSANDS UPON THOUSANDS OF BUILDINGS WITH BRIGHT WINDOWS, LIGHTS TO OUTSHINE THE STARS. UNDERTON SEES NONE OF IT. BUT IN HIS MIND'S EYE HE SEES WHERE CARLOS LIVES. AND SEEING WHERE CARLOS LIVES, HE SEES THE TOKEN.

CLOSE, SO VERY CLOSE.

THE THOUGHT MAKES HIM CLENCH HIS FISTS IN RAGE. HE REMEMBERS ASTEREL. GRIEF GRIPS HIM, RECALLING HOW HE BECAME BLIND.

OH, FOR THE JOYS OF SIGHT!

THE SIGHT OF BLINKING, SHINING SIGNS FOR WHICH ARGON CREATES LAVENDER. ARGON AND MERCURY, MIXED, BRILLIANT BLUE, AND NEON FOR BRIGHT RED-ORANGE. PINK FROM HELIUM, AND FROM KRYPTON, A WHITISH PINK. BEST OF ALL, XENON! FOR A LOW, SILVERY, PURPLE GLOW.

THIS TIME, THE TOKEN WILL BE MINE.

AT LAST I WILL SEE AGAIN!

49

I NEED **THIS** ONE.

WHY?

IT WAS STOLEN.

WHO WOULD DO THAT?

I WAS ABOUT TO GO INTO THE SUBWAY WHEN I DROPPED IT.

I COULDN'T — YOU UNDERSTAND — RETRIEVE IT FOR MYSELF.

THEN I HEARD SOMEONE PICK IT UP. I COULD TELL IT WAS A BOY. I ASKED FOR IT BACK, BUT HE REFUSED, RUDELY.

THAT'S AWFUL.

I FOLLOWED THE BOY BUT COULDN'T CATCH UP WITH HIM BEFORE HE WENT INTO HIS APARTMENT. I COULD HAVE GOTTEN ANOTHER TOKEN, BUT I DECIDED HE NEEDED TO BE REPRIMANDED, TOLD HE ACTED BADLY. AND WOULDN'T IT BE BETTER IF SOMEONE HIS OWN AGE SPOKE TO HIM?

IF I **DO** SPEAK TO HIM, AND HE DOES GIVE IT BACK, CAN I GO TO SCHOOL?

OF COURSE.

SO IT'S THE BOY'S RUDENESS THAT MATTERS, NOT THE TOKEN.

WRONG!

I MUST HAVE THE **EXACT** ONE HE TOOK FROM ME. THAT'S JUSTICE. IT'S YOUR DUTY TO HELP ME SET THINGS RIGHT.

I'LL LET YOUR FATHER KNOW IF I WANT YOU TOMORROW.

WHAT IF THAT BOY USED THE TOKEN?

I TOLD YOU HE DID NOT HAVE IT!

GLAD HE DIDN'T ASK ME, BUT... I'M SURE THAT BOY GOES TO MY SCHOOL....

FROM HER HIDING PLACE, ASTEREL WATCHES THE BLIND MAN AND HIS DOG HEAD DOWN THE STREET. SHE'S SEEN AND HEARD EVERYTHING THAT HAS HAPPENED.

SHOULD I FOLLOW UNDERTON? SHOULD I FOLLOW THE GIRL? COULD **THAT** GIRL BE MY DAUGHTER?

THE POSSIBILITY BRINGS ASTEREL AGONY AND JOY. SHE KNOWS SHE MUST TRY TO FIND THE BOY. THE KURBS' DEADLINE IS FAST APPROACHING, BUT IT WAS ELEVEN YEARS AGO THAT SHE RETURNED THE TOKEN, ONLY TO LOSE HER DAUGHTER.

THE BOY'S GONE. I'LL FOLLOW THE GIRL.

PUBLIC SCHOOL

ALL THIS FUSS OVER A TOKEN!

IN SCHOOL, SARAH SPENDS THE MORNING MULLING OVER WHAT HAS HAPPENED. HOW CAN HER FATHER AND UNDERTON BE FRIENDS? AS FOR THAT BOY, IF SHE COULD GET HIM TO GIVE **HER** THE TOKEN, SHE WOULD NOT HAVE TO MEET UNDERTON AGAIN.

DURING LUNCH, SARAH LOOKS FOR THE BOY IN EARNEST. BUT THE CAFETERIA IS VERY CROWDED, AND AT FIRST SHE CAN'T FIND HIM. SHE SITS WITH HER FRIEND TORY INSTEAD.

WHAT ARE YOU LOOKING AT?

SEE THAT BOY OVER THERE?

SARAH, THERE ARE TEN MILLION BOYS.

THE ONE UNDER THE CLOCK. WITH THAT OTHER BOY.

THAT'S CARLOS JUAREZ. I'VE CALLED HIM FOR HOMEWORK A FEW TIMES. HE'S WITH TOM MARTIN. ALL THEY EVER TALK ABOUT IS AIRPLANES.

HOW COME YOU'RE INTERESTED IN HIM?

JUST CURIOUS.

EXCUSE ME. CARLOS?

HUH?

CAN I TALK TO YOU FOR A MINUTE?

IT'S KIND OF PRIVATE.

THAT'S OKAY. I'LL CATCH YOU LATER.

THE MOMENT SARAH EMERGES FROM SCHOOL, ASTEREL - WHO HAS WAITED ALL DAY FOR HER TO APPEAR - WATCHES INTENTLY. THEN CARLOS COMES OUT OF THE BUILDING. ASTEREL GIVES A START.

THE BOY WITH THE TOKEN!

BUT THE GIRL MOVES AWAY IN ONE DIRECTION, THE BOY IN ANOTHER. ONCE AGAIN ASTEREL IS TORN OVER WHOM TO FOLLOW.

CONSOLING HERSELF WITH THE KNOWLEDGE THAT SHE KNOWS WHERE THE GIRL LIVES, ASTEREL FALLS IN BEHIND THE BOY.

YOU GONNA TELL ME ABOUT THAT GIRL?

SAID HER NAME WAS SARAH.

OH, YEAH, SARAH STUBBS. WHAT DID SHE WANT?

CARLOS BEGINS BY EXPLAINING HOW HE GOT THE TOKEN AND FINISHES WITH SARAH'S ACCUSATION THAT HE STOLE IT.

THAT TRUE? YOU REALLY GOT IT FROM A BIRD?

HONEST! AND IT'S THE SAME AS ANY I EVER SAW.

LET'S SEE IT.

LEFT IT HOME.

HOW'D THAT GIRL KNOW ABOUT IT?

SAID SOME FRIEND OF HERS - A BLIND GUY - TOLD HER.

IF HE WAS BLIND, HOW'D HE KNOW?

DOESN'T MAKE SENSE, DOES IT? AND SHE EVEN SAID SHE'D GIVE ME MONEY FOR IT.

YOU GOING TO HAND IT OVER?

I DON'T KNOW.

UPSET, SARAH REPLACES THE LITTLE BOOK ON THE SHELF, THEN GOES UPSTAIRS. SHE TAKES THE PHOTO OF THE WOMAN SHE THOUGHT WAS HER MOTHER.

SARAH STARTS HER HOMEWORK, THE PHOTO BEFORE HER. FROM TIME TO TIME SHE GAZES AT IT. "IS THIS REALLY MY MOTHER?" SHE KEEPS ASKING HERSELF.

ON TOM'S ROOF...

DO...DO YOU LIVE HERE?

OH, NO. I HAVE A PLACE TO GO...BUT IT'S A LONG WALK AND IT'S VERY COLD OUTSIDE. I COULD TAKE A BUS OR SUBWAY, EXCEPT...

EXCEPT WHAT?

I HAVE NO MONEY.

NEITHER DO I.

YOU WOULDN'T HAVE TO GIVE ME MONEY. IT COULD BE... A TOKEN.

IF I HAD ONE, I'D GIVE IT TO YOU. BUT, HONEST, I DON'T.

THAT'S A DISAPPOINTMENT. HELP ME UP.

WHAT ABOUT YOUR APARTMENT? DO YOU HAVE A TOKEN THERE?

MAYBE.

IF I MET YOU OUTSIDE YOUR DOOR TOMORROW, WOULD YOU GIVE IT TO ME?

I SUPPOSE....

THEN I'LL BE WAITING.

WAIT A MINUTE! WHO ARE YOU?

69

HAVE TO HURRY.... NOW, WHERE WAS THAT TOKEN?

CLICK

NO! SOMEONE'S COMING IN THE DOOR!

WHEW....

WHAT ARE YOU DOING HERE? HOW DID YOU GET IN?

WHO ARE YOU?

YESTERDAY YOU TOOK A TOKEN FROM A BIRD.

THAT TOKEN BELONGS TO ME.

I AM PREPARED TO GIVE YOU THIS WHEN YOU RETURN THAT TOKEN TO ME.

STOP! DON'T MOVE CLOSER TO THE DOOR!

I'M AWARE THAT THIS MUST SEEM STRANGE TO YOU,

BUT YOU HAVE NO CHOICE.

75

NOW CARLOS REMEMBERS THE BUS RIDE HOME FROM THE FAMILY PARTY. HADN'T HE HELD THE TOKEN THEN, AND HADN'T THINGS BECOME BRIGHT? THEY HAD! AND FINDING THE MAGAZINE! IT HAD BEEN WHILE HOLDING THE TOKEN THAT HE SAW **THROUGH** THE COUCH!

WOW...

ASTONISHED, CARLOS REMAINS STANDING IN HIS ROOM, HOLDING THE TOKEN, TRYING TO MAKE SENSE OF WHAT HAS JUST HAPPENED.

THE MAN WHO WANTED THE TOKEN IS **BLIND.**

NO SOONER DOES CARLOS **THINK** OF THE BLIND MAN THAN AN IMAGE - AS CLEAR AS ANY TV PICTURE - COMES INTO HIS HEAD.

AMAZING.

WHAT IS THIS TOKEN?

4TH CHAPTER

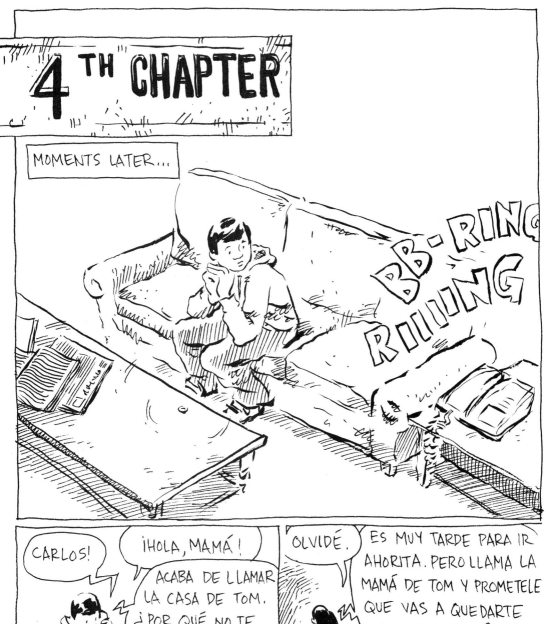

MOMENTS LATER...

BB-RING ROIIING

CARLOS!

¡HOLA, MAMÁ!

ACABA DE LLAMAR LA CASA DE TOM. ¿POR QUÉ NO TE QUEDASTE CON ELLOS?

"HI, MOM!"

"I JUST CALLED TOM'S. WHY DIDN'T YOU STAY WITH THEM?"

OLVIDÉ.

ES MUY TARDE PARA IR AHORITA. PERO LLAMA LA MAMÁ DE TOM Y PROMETELE QUE VAS A QUEDARTE CON ELLOS MAÑANA.

"I FORGOT."

"IT'S TOO LATE TO GO NOW. BUT CALL TOM'S MOTHER AND PROMISE YOU'LL STAY TOMORROW."

LO HARÉ. ¿COME SE SIENTE TIÁ NINA?

MEJOR. ¿SABES QUÉ?

MAÑANA TENGO UNA ENTREVISTA AQUÍ PARA UN TRABAJO.

¡FANTÁSTICO! ¡OJALÁ QUE LO GANES!

"I WILL. HOW'S AUNT NINA?"

"FEELING BETTER. GUESS WHAT?"

"I HAVE A JOB INTERVIEW HERE TOMORROW."

"GREAT! HOPE YOU GET IT!"

BUENO, AMOR. ¿VAS A ESTAR BIEN? SÍ.

TE LLAMARÉ A CASA DE TOM. ADIOS.

"ALL RIGHT, LOVE. YOU GOING TO BE OKAY?" "YEAH."

"I'LL PHONE YOU TOMORROW AT TOM'S." "BYE."

BBRING

HELLO?

MAY I SPEAK TO CARLOS JUAREZ, PLEASE?

SPEAKING.

THIS IS SARAH STUBBS, THE ONE WHO ASKED YOU ABOUT THAT TOKEN. I NEED TO TALK TO YOU ABOUT IT.

WHAT FOR?

81

I'M CLOSE TO THE BREAKING POINT! I MUST HAVE THAT TOKEN!

I BEG YOU...

I HAVE **NEVER** LEARNED **HOW** ASTEREL RETURNS THE TOKEN TO SAFEKEEPING. I NO LONGER CARE. IF I FAIL TO GET THE TOKEN BEFORE THE DEADLINE THIS TIME, I SHALL COME FOR YOU. THEN WE TWO SHALL MAKE A DIRECT APPEAL TO THEM.

TO THE KURBS?

OFFER SARAH?

I WILL OFFER THEM AN EXCHANGE: ESTELLA FOR THE TOKEN.

I WILL NOT BE DENIED ANOTHER YEAR!

GO HOME. I'LL INFORM YOU ABOUT MY PLANS LATER.

EN 24 HRS
L.E.M'S

IN THE STUBBS APARTMENT...

CAN'T STAND THIS WAITING FOR DAD. MAYBE THAT CARLOS... BUT IF I CALL ANOTHER TIME, HE'LL PROBABLY JUST HANG UP AGAIN. I WONDER WHAT HE'D DO IF I WENT TO HIS HOME.

CAN'T THINK OF ANYTHING ELSE TO DO. I'LL WALK, BUT I'LL TAKE SOME BUS FARE, JUST IN CASE.

THAT THEO IS A FOOL. BUT I MUSTN'T PUSH HIM TOO HARD. ALWAYS THE CHANCE HE'LL...

SKOTOS, TO CONTROL STUBBS I HAVE TO ASSERT MY AUTHORITY OVER THE GIRL.

LEAD ME TO STUBBS' CANDY STORE.

MOMENTS AFTER SARAH LEAVES...

RAP RAP RAP

ANY LIGHTS, SKOTOS?

BARK

NONE? THEN WHERE ARE THEY?

89

THIS SARAH IS OKAY.

COOL. I'M PUTTING OUR PHONE NEXT TO MY BED. IF YOU NEED ANYTHING, ANYTIME, CALL.

OKAY.

I MEAN IT. **ANYTIME.**

ALL RIGHT. TELL ME WHAT'S HAPPENING.

SARAH TELLS CARLOS WHAT SHE KNOWS ABOUT UNDERTON.

I WISH I KNEW WHY MY FATHER HAS BEEN GIVING HIM MONEY.

THEN SHE TELLS HIM ABOUT HER DISCOVERIES THAT DAY CONCERNING HER MOTHER'S PICTURE.

YOU MEAN, YOU'VE NEVER SEEN YOUR MOTHER?

NEVER.

WELL, I HARDLY EVER SEE MY FATHER.

I TRIED TO TALK TO MY FATHER. HE JUST RAN OFF. I COULDN'T JUST SIT HOME. SO I DECIDED TO COME OVER.

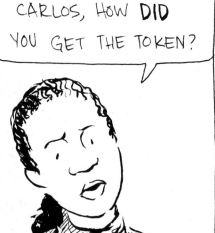

CARLOS, HOW **DID** YOU GET THE TOKEN?

ASTEREL?

WHO ARE YOU?

THEODORE BITNER... ELEVEN YEARS OLDER, HEAD SHAVEN, A BEARD... BUT STILL THEODORE BITNER.

THEO?

YES.

NO WONDER I COULDN'T FIND YOU. I SUPPOSE YOU TOOK A FALSE NAME, TOO.

YES. STUBBS.

STUBBS' CANDY CARNIVAL.

HOW DID YOU FIND OUT?

UNDERTON WAS AT YOUR DOOR THIS MORNING. AND TODAY, AFTER ALL THESE YEARS, I SAW ESTELLA.

IT'S TIME FOR ME TO CONFESS.

ENTER, THEO.

WHAT HAPPENED?

EVERYTHING BECAME BRIGHT.

EXACTLY.

NOW CLOSE YOUR FINGERS OVER IT AND THINK ABOUT A PERSON.

LIKE—MY FATHER?

SURE.

I SEE HIM!

WHERE IS HE?

HE'S COMING DOWN A STREET. IT'S NOT FAR FROM WHERE WE LIVE. HE MUST BE GOING HOME.

NEAT, ISN'T IT?

CARLOS, I THINK THERE'S SOMEONE WITH HIM.

WHO?

CAN'T TELL. IT'S OUT OF FOCUS.

WHAT MAKES IT DO THAT?

BEATS ME. THINK YOUR FATHER KNOWS?

I GUESS. I JUST WISH I KNEW WHO HE WAS WITH.

MAYBE YOU HAVE TO KNOW WHO YOU'RE LOOKING AT BEFORE IT GETS CLEAR.

COULD IT BE THAT UNDERTON GUY?

BETTER CHECK.

96

105

SPONGY AND SHRILL. SHADOW AND SMOKE. PEOPLE SEE THEM ALL THE TIME WITHOUT REALIZING.

WHAT'S UNDERTON HAVE TO DO WITH THEM?

ESTELLA HEARS THE TRUTH ABOUT UNDERTON.

MY FATHER HAS BEEN PAYING HIM MONEY FOR YEARS.

IN RETURN HE PROMISES TO PROTECT YOUR FATHER FROM ME.

WHY?

SARAH LEARNS HOW ASTEREL AND THEO MET, ABOUT THEIR LOVE, MARRIAGE, AND CHILD.

MAYBE MY FATHER DIDN'T KNOW WHERE YOU WERE.

HE CAME TO ME TONIGHT.

BUT WHEN YOU HAD THE TOKEN, COULDN'T YOU SEE ME?

I HAVE THE POWER TO SEE WHO HAS THE TOKEN. TO SEE ANYONE ELSE, I MUST KNOW **EXACTLY** WHAT THEY LOOK LIKE. YOUR FATHER TOOK ON A DISGUISE TO PREVENT MY SEEING HIM.

AS FOR YOU, I LOOKED FOR YOU EVERYWHERE I WENT. BUT THE TWO-DAY-OLD BABY I KNEW NO LONGER EXISTS, DOES SHE?

UNDERTON TOOK CARE NEVER TO COME HERE. THIS MORNING HE DID, AND WHEN I FOLLOWED HIM I SAW YOU FOR THE FIRST TIME.

YOU KEPT THE TOKEN UNTIL I WAS BORN. YOU COULD HAVE RETURNED IT SOONER AND NONE OF THIS WOULD HAVE HAPPENED.

WHY DID YOU KEEP IT?

BECAUSE I NEEDED TO DO THIS.

WHAT DOES THAT DO?

ESTELLA — FROM THE MOMENT THAT TOKEN TOUCHED YOU —

RING RING

IS THIS SARAH?

YES.

THIS IS UNDERTON. LISTEN CAREFULLY, FOR I SHALL NOT REPEAT MYSELF. I KNOW THAT YOU, OR PERHAPS THAT BOY, OR PERHAPS BY NOW EVEN ASTEREL, HAS THAT TOKEN.

BUT IF YOU WANT TO SEE YOUR FATHER ALIVE, I **MUST** HAVE IT.

CLICK

109

110

BUT IF I EXPLAINED IT WAS MY FATHER, WOULDN'T THAT HELP?

ESTELLA, KURBS DON'T FAIL TO PUNISH THOSE WHO OFFEND THEM OR THEIR RULES.

OUT THERE NOW? **ON THE STREET?**

EVERYWHERE.

GOOD THING YOU HAVE SAFETY BARS.

BARS MIGHT KEEP YOU OR ME IN. NOT THE KURBS.

EXTRA TIME HAS NEVER BEEN GRANTED.

WHERE CAN I MEET THEM?

THE KURBS? THERE ARE PROBABLY SOME RIGHT OUTSIDE THE STORE.

CAN'T WE EVEN TRY?

I CAN'T RISK SACRIFICING THE CITY FOR THEO.

BUT HE'S MY FATHER!

I WISH IT COULD BE OTHERWISE.

IT CANNOT.

I'LL MAKE SOME TEA. CARLOS, GIVE ME A HAND.

CARLOS, I HAVE TO DO **SOMETHING.**

119

UNDERTON RETURNS TO THE WATERFRONT....

COO COO CLUCK COO COO COO

SKOTOS! I KNOW WHERE THOSE CHILDREN ARE!

HURRY! WE CAN CATCH THEM!

UNDERGROUND...

KURBS! MILLIONS OF THEM!

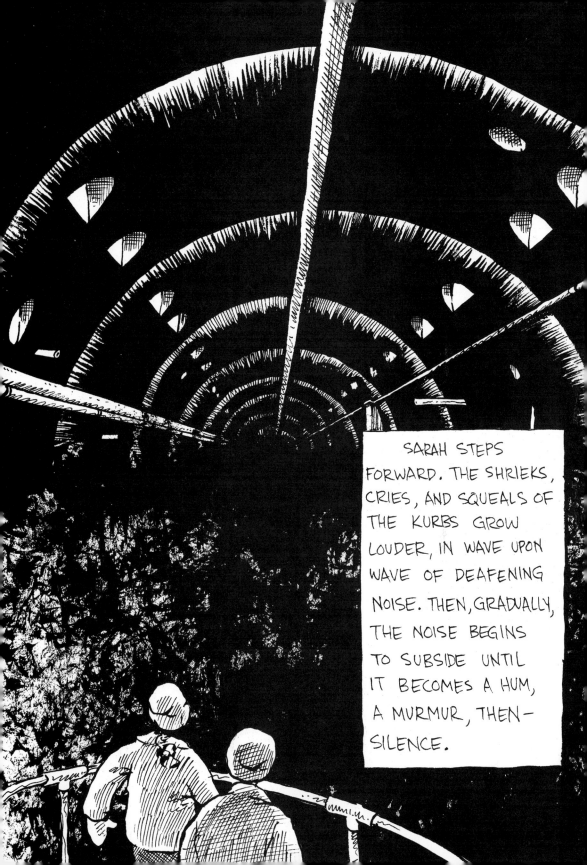

SARAH STEPS FORWARD. THE SHRIEKS, CRIES, AND SQUEALS OF THE KURBS GROW LOUDER, IN WAVE UPON WAVE OF DEAFENING NOISE. THEN, GRADUALLY, THE NOISE BEGINS TO SUBSIDE UNTIL IT BECOMES A HUM, A MURMUR, THEN— SILENCE.

SOMEONE FROM THE CITY HAS DISCOVERED THE **POWER** OF THE TOKEN. HE'S TRIED HARD TO STEAL IT.

THIS MAN'S NAMED UNDERTON. NOT ONLY DID HE TRY TO STEAL THE TOKEN, HE'S STOLEN MY FATHER AND IS HOLDING HIM HOSTAGE. UNLESS THE TOKEN IS GIVEN TO UNDERTON, HE'LL DESTROY MY FATHER.

OUR TRIBUTE! OUR TRIBUTE! OUR TRIBUT OUR TRIB

I NEED THE TOKEN TO FIND HIM AND SAVE HIM. I PROMISE THAT ONCE HE'S FREE, I'LL BRING IT RIGHT BACK.

PLEASE, I NEED MORE TIME.

RRRRRRRRRRRR

RROARR

HOW DARE YOU COME HERE, CHILD!

THIS PLACE IS FORBIDDEN TO PEOPLE. YOU TEST OUR ANGER, AND WE TELL YOU, CHILD, THAT NEVER IN ALL THE YEARS HAVE WE EXTENDED THE DEADLINE. NOT BY A DAY. NOT AN HOUR. NOT ONE SECOND. NEVER.

THE LAND YOU PEOPLE LIVE ON BELONGS TO US, THE KURBS. IT HAS ONLY BEEN LOANED TO YOU. IF YOU FAIL TO FULFILL THE RITUAL CYCLE OF ACKNOWLEDGMENT, WE WILL TAKE OUR ISLAND BACK. O CHILD, YOU WHO HAVE THE TOKEN, LISTEN!

THE RITUAL INSISTS THE TOKEN SHALL BE IN ITS REQUIRED PLACE OF SAFEKEEPING BY THE TWENTY-FIRST DAY OF DECEMBER, AT THE STROKE OF NOON, OR YOU PEOPLE SHALL SUFFER THE CONSEQUENCES! THE DEADLINE IS TODAY! BE WARNED!

WHAT'S HAPPENING?

I THINK THEY'RE SENDING US AWAY.

GUESS WE BETTER GO.

TWENTY MINUTES OF WALKING BRINGS THEM TO A MASSIVE DOOR. AS THEY APPROACH, THE DOOR OPENS AND THEY PASS THROUGH. THEY ARE BACK IN THE ABANDONED EIGHTEENTH STREET SUBWAY STATION.

STAY WHERE YOU ARE! THERE'S NO WAY OFF THIS TRAIN!

WE'RE GOING TOO FAST. WE CAN'T GET OFF.

I WANT THAT TOKEN NOW!

HE'S COMING!

LET'S GET TO THE FRONT END! MAYBE HE CAN'T FOLLOW US.

THE TRAIN IS FIVE CARS LONG. SARAH AND CARLOS HAVE TO OPEN AND CLOSE THE DOORS OF EACH CAR BEFORE REACHING THE NEXT. BY THE TIME THEY GET TO THE FRONT CAR, THEY HAVE PASSED STILL ANOTHER STATION.

AT THE FINAL CAR THEY LOOK BACK.

HE'S STILL COMING!

WHAT'S THIS DOOR? THE DRIVER'S BOX! MAYBE WE CAN STOP THE TRAIN AT THE NEXT STATION.

CARLOS, WHICH LEVER?

I DON'T KNOW.

OH OH! HE'S IN THE NEXT CAR!

ONE OF THESE MUST BE A THROTTLE.

THE OTHER SHOULD BE THE BRAKE.

TRY TO KEEP HIM OUT! I'LL TRY TO STOP US.

129

130

WE'RE SEEKING A TOKEN.

WHEN YOU SEE ONE, YOU ARE TO PICK IT UP AND BRING IT TO ME.

GO! TAKE IT TO YOUR MASTER! GO!

WHAT DID YOU DO THAT FOR?

IT WASN'T THE IMPORTANT ONE. IT WAS THAT EXTRA I HAD.

YOU SURE?

ABSOLUTELY.

BETTER TEST IT.

IT WORKS.

YOU SCARED ME.

C'MON. LET'S GET TO YOUR FRIEND'S.

134

SKOTOS RETURNS TO WHERE UNDERTON HAS BEEN WAITING....

ANSWER ME, SKOTOS!

WHERE ARE THOSE CHILDREN?

YOU DIDN'T BRING THEM, DID YOU?

WHIMPER

CHEATED!

TRICKED!

DESTROYED!

YOU'VE LET THEM GET AWAY!

YOU'VE GONE OVER TO THEM, HAVEN'T YOU, YOU FOOL!

GET AWAY FROM ME.

FAILED ME WHEN I NEEDED YOU MOST!

THE ONE I TRUSTED MOST. MY ONLY FRIEND.

GO!

I DON'T WANT YOU NEAR ME AGAIN! I DON'T NEED YOU!

GO TO YOUR FRIENDS!

WHAT ABOUT ALL THREE JUMPING OUT AT HIM. THEN EACH OF US GO A DIFFERENT WAY. HE WON'T KNOW WHICH ONE TO GO AFTER. HE'LL HAVE TO GUESS.

HE'S GOOD AT GUESSING RIGHT.

ANYWAY, WE HAVE TO GET HER FATHER FAST. AND WE DON'T EVEN KNOW WHERE HE IS.

SHHH!

HE'S RIGHT OUTSIDE.

SARAH — I KNOW YOU ARE THERE.

I ADMIT IT:

YOU HAVE DEFEATED ME.

SARAH! DO YOU HAVE ANY IDEA HOW MUCH I'VE ACHED FOR THE JOYS OF SIGHT? DO YOU KNOW HOW HARD IT IS FOR ME — WHO ONCE MADE VISIONS OF LIGHT THAT TURNED NIGHT INTO DAY — HOW HARD TO SEE ONLY AN ENDLESS, ACHING DARKNESS?

I BEG YOU, GIVE ME SIGHT FOR JUST AN HOUR'S TIME.

TEN MINUTES.

ONE MINUTE.

138

139

8TH CHAPTER

THE NEXT INSTANT...

OUR AIRPLANE!

WHAT ARE YOU TALKING ABOUT?

WE CAN **FLY** AFTER HIM! FOLLOW HIM!

HOW? WE DON'T EXACTLY HAVE JET ENGINES LYING ABOUT HERE.

145

9TH CHAPTER

MEANWHILE...

CARLOS!

ONE LAST BURST! ONE MORE!

THE BOAT REACHES LIBERTY ISLAND....

UMM... DECIDED NOT TO STAY.

WHAT HAPPENS NEXT?

WITHOUT THE TOKEN THE CITY FREEZES.

AND THE KURBS TAKE BACK THE ISLAND.

DARK CLOUDS BEGIN TO PILE UP, OBLITERATING THE SUN. IT'S AS IF NIGHT HAD DOUBLED BACK, HOLDING DAY OFF ENTIRELY. THE TEMPERATURE BEGINS TO PLUMMET.

WHY DID YOU KEEP DOING ALL THOSE THINGS FOR UNDERTON?

I WAS AFRAID OF LOSING YOU.

WHAT ABOUT THAT PICTURE... THE ONE OVER YOUR DESK. YOU SAID IT WAS MY MOTHER.

I HAD TO SHOW YOU SOMETHING.

BUT I WAS AFRAID TO SHOW YOU A REAL PICTURE. I GOT THAT ONE IN A JUNK SHOP.

IS ASTEREL MY REAL MOTHER?

YES.

I LIKE HER.

SO DO I.

BY THE TIME THE BOAT REACHES THE DOCK, A STORM HAS BEGUN, A DRIVING, SLEETING STORM THAT COVERS EVERY SURFACE OF THE BOAT WITH A CRUST OF SLIPPERY ICE.

THE THREE BARELY WAIT FOR THE GANG-PLANK TO BE LET DOWN BEFORE THEY RUSH OFF INTO THE STREET.

THE WEATHER WORSENS.
WHIRLING SNOW MAKES IT ALL
BUT IMPOSSIBLE TO SEE. VICIOUS
WINDS CAREEN UP AND DOWN THE
STREETS, BUFFETING ALL WHO
DARE TO BRAVE THEM. SO DARK IS
IT THAT STREET LAMPS HAVE
COME ON. LAMPPOSTS RATTLE.
HYDRANTS FREEZE. PEOPLE
WALK HUNCHED OVER, HOLDING
DOWN COATS, TRYING TO INSULATE
THEMSELVES FROM THE CUTTING
EDGES OF THE WIND.

TRAFFIC IS AT A CRAWL. THE
INCESSANT GRINDING OF FROZEN
AUTO ENGINES FILLS THE AIR
WITH GROANS THAT SET TEETH
ON EDGE.

STUBBS, SARAH, AND CARLOS STRUGGLE DOWN INTO THE NEAREST SUBWAY. THEY WAIT FOR A TRAIN. IT IS TOO COLD FOR TALK. BETWEEN THE TRACKS POOLS OF WATER TURN TO ICE.

IN THE SUBWAY RIDERS ARE QUIETER THAN NORMAL, BUT THEY MUTTER ABOUT THE LACK OF HEAT. EVERY BREATH IS CLOUDED WITH COLD. HANDS ARE WRUNG. FEET TAP.

MINUTE BY MINUTE THE COLD DEEPENS.

THE CITY IS FREEZING.

179

THE LAST CHAPTER

THAT NIGHT... CARLOS, AS HE HAD PROMISED HIS MOTHER, IS AT TOM'S APARTMENT. HE AND TOM HAVE ALREADY DECIDED NOT TO TELL THE ADULTS WHAT HAPPENED, BECAUSE THEY ARE CERTAIN NO GROWN-UP WOULD BELIEVE IT.

AFTER DINNER, CARLOS'S MOTHER CALLS.

¿ADIVINA QUE PASÓ?

NO PUEDO.

"GUESS WHAT'S HAPPENED?"

"CAN'T."

ME OFRECIERON EL TRABAJO AQUÍ.

¿EN EL CAMPO?

EXACTAMENTE LO QUE QUIERES.

BUENO, MAMÁ, NO ESTOY MUY SEGURO QUE QUIERO IR.

¡CARLOS! ¿QUE HA PASADO CONTIGO?

ESTAN PASANDO COSAS INTERESANTES.

"I GOT A JOB OFFER OUT HERE."

"IN THE COUNTRY?"

"JUST WHAT YOU WANTED."

"YEAH, WELL, MA, I'M NOT SO SURE I WANT TO GO."

"CARLOS! WHAT'S COME OVER YOU?"

"THERE'S SOME INTERESTING STUFF GOING ON...."

SARAH GAVE THAT SPECIAL TOKEN TO THE DOG BY MISTAKE, RIGHT? BEFORE YOU GOT HERE LAST NIGHT. ISN'T THAT WHAT YOU SAID?

RIGHT.

WE'RE PRETTY LUCKY UNDERTON DIDN'T GET IT.

OKAY, THEN HOW COME, IF SHE **DIDN'T** HAVE THE TOKEN, SHE WAS ABLE TO DO ALL THAT STUFF?

YOU KNOW, LIKE SEEING THINGS IN HER HEAD, GIVING POWER TO THE PLANE? ALL THAT STUFF. THAT'S WHAT I DON'T UNDERSTAND. DO YOU KNOW WHAT I'M SAYING?

YOU'RE RIGHT.

AFTER SARAH GAVE THE TOKEN TO SKOTOS, I COULDN'T DO ANYTHING WITH THE TOKEN.

BUT SHE COULD.

WELL?

I'M NOT SURE. LET'S ASK HER AT SCHOOL TOMORROW.

THE NEXT WEEKEND, IN ASTEREL'S CAVE...

WHAT SHALL I BE NEXT YEAR? DOGCATCHER? FIREFIGHTER? ICE-CREAM VENDOR?

MA?

HOW **DID** I DO ALL THAT STUFF?

BECAUSE YOU ARE MY DAUGHTER, ESTELLA, AND ALL MY POWERS ARE YOUR POWERS.

THEY ARE?

REMEMBER, IN YOUR FATHER'S HOUSE, JUST BEFORE YOU AND CARLOS RAN OFF, I PRESSED THE TOKEN TO YOUR FOREHEAD?

THAT IS EXACTLY WHAT I HAD TO DO RIGHT AFTER YOU WERE BORN, THE REASON I HAD HELD ONTO THE TOKEN. ONCE I ANOINTED YOU, I GAVE YOU ALL MY POWERS BECAUSE, WELL, AFTER ALL, YOU ARE MY DAUGHTER.

NOW YOU KNOW HOW I CAME TO BE THE SEARCHER OF THE TOKEN. IT WAS MY MOTHER BEFORE ME, AS IT WAS HER MOTHER BEFORE HER, WHO DID THE SAME. OH, WE COME FROM AN ANCIENT PEOPLE, ESTELLA. SO SOMEDAY, WHAT I DO, YOU TOO SHALL DO.

ME? AM I REALLY TO BE LIKE YOU?

OH, YES, THE SAME. BUT YOURSELF, TOO.

DO I GET TO CHOOSE WHAT I WANT TO BE EACH AND EVERY YEAR?

YES.

BUT NOT FOR A WHILE, RIGHT?

NOT FOR A WHILE.